Gardeners' Calendar

EDITED BY GRAHAM CLARKE

Produced specially for Damart
by Ward Lock Ltd, 82 Gower Street, London WC1E 6EQ

Text filmset in Plantin
by Paul Hicks Limited
Middleton, Manchester

Printed in Belgium
ISBN 0 7063 4271 2

Acknowledgements

The publishers are grateful to the following agencies for granting permission to
reproduce the following colour photographs:
Harry Smith Horticultural Photographic Collection
(pp. 2, 7, 19, 22, 31, 38, 39 and back cover);
Pat Brindley (pp. 10, 15, 27, 43 and 46).
The publishers are also grateful to Arthur Billitt of Clack's Farm in providing the
locations for the photographs on the front cover and on p. 35, which were taken by
Bob Challinor.

Front cover : A colourful border at Clack's Farm
p. 2 : Cottage garden in Essex
p. 3 : *Fremontia californica*
Back cover : Lawn and borders.

CONTENTS

The following items are discussed:
Weather; Trees and shrubs; Flowers;
Vegetables; and Topical tips.

January

WEATHER AND THE GARDENER

Daytime temperatures in winter depend greatly on the direction of the wind; the warmth from the limited sunshine is too weak to make much difference. Northerly winds will always bring cold weather because the air reaching Britain has originated in arctic regions. Easterly winds can be even colder because they come from the winter 'pole' of low temperature in northern Siberia; even a southerly wind which draws in air from a continental source can be cold in winter and is often associated with some of the heaviest snowfalls in southern England. Westerly winds are typical of the milder winters which are usually very wet with little or no snow except on the highest ground.

The drop in temperature from day to night will not be great in cloudy windy weather, and the hardest frosts will occur if the night sky is clear and the wind light.

TREES AND SHRUBS

COLOURFUL PLANTS THIS MONTH Trees, shrubs and climbers which produce colour this month include those with colourful bark, such as cornus (dogwoods); and certain plants which commence flowering, such as *Chimonanthus praecox* (winter sweet), *Erica carnea* and *E. × darleyensis* (heaths and heathers) varieties, *Garrya elliptica* (silk tassel bush), *Jasminum nudiflorum* (winter jasmine), *Lonicera frangrantissima* (shrubby honeysuckle) and *Viburnum × bodnantense* varieties and *V. tinus*.

PRUNING The start of the new year is a good time to examine existing trees, shrubs and climbers and to remove from them dead, diseased, damaged or unwanted wood. Use sharp secateurs or pruning saw and ensure the cuts are made cleanly and leave no snags. Paint large cuts with a proprietory bitumen compound to prevent entry of disease. Discard the pruned shoots and branches.

FLOWERS

HARDY BORDER PLANTS Plan new borders. Aim for a continuity of flower colour throughout the year. Intersperse flowering plants with those valued for their handsome leaves e.g. veratrum, *Salvia argentea* macleaya and *Stachys lanata*.

Skimmia japonica berries in winter

Dig new sites deeply; ideally by double digging them. Work old manure into the bottom spit and remove any roots you find of perennial weeds such as bindweed, docks, thistles, nettles and couch grass.

ALPINES Remove accumulations of autumn-fallen leaves that have built up round the stems of rock plants, for continual dampness caused will rot fleshy stems.

Cover felty, woolly-leaved plants with panes of glass or Perspex supported on wires clipped to their edges. This keeps off winter moisture which can rot the foliage.

BULBS Spread slug pellets round winter-flowering bulbs such as *Cyclamen coum, Iris histrioides* and galanthus, where plants are growing in soggy soil heavily populated by slugs

Set fine string or cotton over patches of *Crocus imperati* and other winter flowering kinds, to keep birds from tearing the petals.

Look over stored gladiolus corms and reject any which are soft and diseased.

VEGETABLES

JANUARY SOWINGS Sow mustard and cress now. These are useful salad vegetables at any time of year. It is better to grow them separately because the cress takes three or four days longer than the mustard to reach maturity.

STARTING POTATOES Obtain potato seed as early in January as possible. Set them up in trays with the rose end upwards; this is the one which has the greater number of 'eyes'. Place in warm conditions and full light so that slow sprouting can take place. When the sprouts are well visible, reduce their number to two to improve the size of the earliest tubers.

TOPICAL TIPS

FROST PROTECTION Ensure that any plants you suspect to be tender are given protection from severe weather. Those outdoors can be covered with piles of dry straw or bracken held down with wire netting; plants in greenhouses can be covered with sheets of newspaper at night and the house double-glazed with polythene.

SEED ORDER Now is the time to choose this year's vegetable and flower seeds from the catalogues. Send your order in early to avoid disappointment.

February

WEATHER AND THE GARDENER

If the winter is wet, and especially if the previous summer was also rainy and lacking in sunshine, then it is always wise at the end of February to check the pH and nitrogen levels in the garden soil to see if extra spring dressings are advisable.

The other feature of garden climate which is important at this time of the year is the soil temperature, which is often the ultimate decider as to whether the spring is early or late. Soil temperatures are always at their lowest in early February and will be likely to be below average if there has been a succession of nights with hard frosts and no snow cover.

TREES AND SHRUBS

COLOURFUL PLANTS THIS MONTH Trees, shrubs and climbers in flower this month include the forms of *Magnolia campbellii,* certain prunus (ornamental cherries, peaches and apricots) in sheltered positions, some rhododendrons and camellias, some cornus (dogwoods), *Daphne mezereum* and *D. odora,* various ericas (heaths and heathers), *Garrya elliptica* (silk tassel bush), forms of hamamelis (witch hazel), *Jasminum nudiflorum* (winter jasmine), various loniceras (shrubby honeysuckles), *Mahonia japonica* (syn. *M. bealei)* and several viburnums.

PRUNING Cut back shoots of summer-flowering clematis to about 1m (3¼ft) and remove completely all dead growths. Prune side shoots of *Vitis vinifera* (ornamental grape vines) and wisteria to one or two buds and generally tidy these climbers to keep them in shape and within bounds.

PLANTING Plant trees and shrubs whenever 'open' weather conditions allow or store plants in a frost-proof place until they can be set out. Prepare the ground thoroughly for all trees, shrubs and climbers, and with the latter make sure the supports up which they are to grow - pergola, arch, trellis, old trees, or wires against a wall - are securely in position.

FLOWERS

HARDY BORDER PLANTS Remove any tall dead flowered stems of vigorous

plants such as echinops, lupins and helianthus that were not cut back in autumn.

Continue scattering slug bait round fleshy crownèd plants such as delphiniums and macleayas.

Check over canes used to support tall growing plants. Clean off mud and dip bases in green Cuprinol to protect them from rot.

Take root cuttings of anchusas, oriental poppies, phlox, romneyas and dicentras.

ALPINES Plant containerized species and varieties when the weather is mild and the soil free from frost. Set feature shrubs such as *Juniperus communis* 'Hibernica' at the foot of an outcrop to provide an intriguing 'punctuation mark'.

Tread round newly planted alpines after heavy frost, to press soil back round their roots.

BULBS Plant the single De Caen and semi-double or double forms of *Anemone coronaria* 5cm (2in) deep and apart in generous groups in a sheltered, sunny or lightly shaded part of the garden. These will bloom in early summer.

VEGETABLES

FEBRUARY SOWINGS Cloches should be put into position early in February, so that the soil underneath has a chance to dry out and possibly warm up. Then one or more of the following crops can be sown: cabbage or early summer cauliflower for planting outside, early carrot (such as the variety Amsterdam Forcing), lettuce, peas and radish. Perhaps not the most universally popular vegetable, broad beans are certainly one of the first to be harvested in the new season, and can be sown in February or March.

TOPICAL TIPS

DIGGING Try to complete any rough digging this month so that the soil can settle before final cultivations.

FINAL CULTIVATIONS Where early sowings are to be made, the soil can now be broken down to a fairly fine tilth with a garden fork, and a little general fertilizer worked in.

CHECK FOR LOSSES If a hard winter has killed off plants in the garden, do a stock check and re-order to fill any gaps.

Early spring display in a conservatory

March

WEATHER AND THE GARDENER

March is traditionally supposed to come in like a lion and to go out like a lamb, but this is not always true as far as strong winds are concerned. It is better to interpret this old saying as that in most years, March brings the first real signs of spring. Spring in the garden comes earliest in the far south-west and latest in the north-east, with the west coastal regions always being ahead of the east. Another important factor is the height of the garden above sea level, for spring is about three days later for every 30m (100ft) increase in height, and a southern facing slope always earlier than one which is north facing.

Remember also that spring flowers depend on "March winds and April showers", the purpose of the winds being to help to dry out the top layers of the seed-bed so that the gardener can create a good tilth.

TREES AND SHRUBS

COLOURFUL PLANTS THIS MONTH Among those in flower this month will be some acer (maples), magnolias, prunus (ornamental cherries), rhododendrons and azaleas, salix (willows), sorbus (mountain ash), camellias, chaenomeles (Japanese quince), *Corylopsis pauciflora, Daphne mezereum,* various ericas (heaths and heathers), forsythia, hamamelis (witch hazel), mahonia, osmanthus and *Viburnum tinus.*

PRUNING Remove old wood from plants that have flowered during the winter, such as *Chimonanthus praecox* (winter sweet), *Lonicera fragrantissima* (shrubby honeysuckle), viburnums, *Jasminum nudiflorum* (winter jasmine). Also remove some growths from winter coloured stemmed plants, such as cornus (dogwoods) and salix (willow), to encourage new, brightly coloured shoots. Remove dead flower heads of winter flowering ericas (heaths and heathers).

Cut out shoots, to within about 5 cm (2in) of old wood, from plants that flower in summer on new growths, such as *Buddleia davidii.*

Pruning of hybrid tea roses may be hard, medium or light depending on the growth of the bush and the purpose for which it is required. In general, however, prune all main growths to within four or five buds from the base, and side shoots to two or three buds, and remove dead or diseased wood.

With floribundas, cut back new shoots to about one third their length, older stems to about half their length, and old wood with new growth to two or three buds from the base.

PLANTING If possible, complete the planting of all new hardy trees, shrubs and climbers. Evergreens, and plants such as lavandula (lavender), rosmarinus (rosemary), hydrangea, cistus (rock rose) and santolina which are not fully hardy until established, are also planted at the end of ' this month or the beginning of the next.

SOIL CULTIVATION Hoe the soil shallowly around trees, shrubs and climbers, taking care not to damage any roots near the surface, and apply a 5cm (2in) layer of mulching material, such as well rotted compost, peat, shredded bark or similar material, with the addition of a general purpose slow-acting fertilizer, such as Growmore. Use a peat mulch for acid loving plants such as rhododendrons, azaleas and ericas.

FLOWERS

HARDY BORDER PLANTS Take 8-10 (3-4in) long basal cuttings of lupins, delphiniums and border chrysanthemums. Cut them away from the clump, with a sharp knife, and remove the lower leaves to retain a healthy growing point. Insert them to half their depth 10cm (4in) apart round the edge of a 13cm (5in) pot of equal parts peat and sharp sand mix. Water in and root in a warm lightly shaded place, such as a heated frame.

Mulch round plants if the weather warms up, with well decomposed manure or old garden compost. Spread a 5cm (2in) thick layer over the soil to insulate the roots from summer heat and provide a downward flow of nutrients to the roots.

ALPINES Divide congested clumps of thyme, campanula, achillea and other summer flowering plants. Split crowns into nicely rooted pieces 5 - 8cm (2 - 3in) across and replant them 15 cm (6in) apart in gritty rich soil consisting of equal parts loam, peat and stone chippings or sharp sand.

Spread slug bait round newly emerging hostas and other fleshy stemmed plants that slugs can ruin by nibbling holes in the leaves.

BLUBS Plant summer-flowering bulbs. Gladioli, specially the grandiflora hybrids with their 90cm (3ft) stems, can be set 8cm (3in) deep and 15cm (6in) apart. The smaller butterfly and primulinus hybrids are best planted only 5cm (2in) deep.

Feed naturalized bulbs carpeting rough-grass areas by scattering a balanced fertilizer high in potash, such as Phostrogen, to stimulate strong growth for the coming year.

Remove faded blooms of earlier flowered bulbs to stop seed formation depriving plants of energy needed for making new growth.

VEGETABLES

SOWING AND PLANTING GUIDE

Vegetable	Sowing/ Planting depth	Planting/ Transplanting period	Spacing between plants	Spacing between rows	Recommended varieties
Brussels sprouts	2cm (¾in)	May/June	60cm (24in)	75cm (30in)	Peer Gynt, Rampart
Cabbage	2cm (¾in)	May	45cm (18in)	45cm (18in)	Hispi, Golden Acre
Carrot	12mm (½in)	—	8cm (3in)	30cm (12in)	Early Nantes, Amsterdam Forcing
Celery	In pots or boxes in greenhouse	May/June	23cm (9in)	23cm (9in)	Solid White, Golden Self-Blanching
Leeks	12mm (½in)	June/July	15cm (6in)	30cm (12in)	Lyon-Prizetaker, Musselburgh
Lettuce	2cm (¾in)	June	30cm (12in)	30cm (12in)	Fortune, Salad Bowl, Webbs Wonderful
Onion (sets)	—	March	10-15cm (4-6in)	30cm (12in)	Sturon
Onion (seed)	12mm (½in)	—	10cm (4in)	30cm (12in)	Ailsa Craig, Solidity
Parsnip	2.5cm (1in)	—	10-15cm (4-6in)	30cm (12in)	Tender and True, White Gem
Pea	2cm (¾in)	—	2.5cm (1in)	60cm (24in)	Feltham First, Early Onward
Radish	12mm (½in)	—	2.5cm (1in)	15-23cm (6-9in)	French Breakfast, Cherry Belle
Potato	10cm (4in)	March	30cm (12in)	60cm (24in)	Pentland Javelin, Pentland Crown

The ever popular daffodil: *Narcissus* 'Carlton'

TOPICAL TIPS

WATER WALL PLANTS Soil borders adjacent to walls receive very little rain water and are often dry. Give them copious supplies of water now, particularly if wall-trained trees and shrubs are being grown.

PATH LAYING The frost should have finished lifting paths now and these can be repaired and new ones laid. Bed flagstones on a 10cm (4in) layer of sand, or lay concrete paths over a 10cm (4in) bed of hardcore.

April

WEATHER AND THE GARDENER

Although the increasing warmth of the sun and the rising soil and air temperatures promote growth in the garden in April, everything can be brought to a halt by one night of frost. Spring frosts are always a major threat when the wind comes from a northerly direction, when the sky clears and the wind dies away at dusk, especially when the soil surface is dry.

The most efficient defence against spring frost in the garden is some form of electrical soil heating, but a glass or plastic cover can provide some limited protection against all but the more severe frosts.

April should see the last of the spring frosts in most gardens in southern England, but the dangerous years are those when both March and April have been very dry months, in which case there is a serious risk of a frost in May.

TREES AND SHRUBS

COLOURFUL PLANTS THIS MONTH Those in flower this month include some forms of amelanchier, magnolia, malus (crabs), prunus (cherries, peaches, apricots, etc.), berberris (barberies), camellias, chaenomeles (Japanese quince), corylopsis, cytisus (broom), daphne, erica (heaths and heathers), forsythia (golden bell bush), *Kerria japonica* (Jew's mallow), mahonia, *Osmanthus delavayi*, pieris, rhododendrons (including azaleas), ribes (flowering currants), spiraea, viburnum, and clematis species.

PRUNING Complete pruning of plants that have flowered earlier in the year and those which flower in summer on new wood. Remove straggly branches of evergreens such as lavandula (lavander), euonymus (spindle tree), and *Magnolia grandiflora*.

PLANTING This is a good month to plant, or transplant, broad leaved evergreens. Plant pot-grown climbers such as wisteria, lonicera (honeysuckle), vitis (ornamental vines), and pot shrubs such as ceanothus and jasminum (jasmine). Water in newly set out plants, and continue regular watering during dry weather.

ROSES Apply a proprietary rose fertilizer at the recommended rate to established roses and lightly hoe it into the soil. All roses benefit from applications of liquid fertilizers at intervals from spring to late summer, provided the soil is damp. If dry, apply plain water a day beforehand. Remove weeds at the same time as feeding.

FLOWERS

HARDY BORDER PLANTS Many plants can be divided and rejuvenated now. Split up large clumps, that are becoming overgrown and flowering poorly, of the following: scabious, knifophia (red hot poker), helianthus (sunflowers) and helenium.

Continue staking leggy plants that are making strong growth. Use canes and string, or twiggy pea sticks.

Watch out for developing colonies of greenfly on soft shoot tips. If seen, spray with systemic insecticide in the late afternoon when bees and other pollinating insects have gone home.

ALPINES Continue planting containerized plants.

Work a mixture of equal parts moist peat and loamy garden soil among the crowns of cushion saxifrages and other spreading, shallow-rooted plants on light soil, to conserve moisture in summer and prevent leaves browning at the edges in dry weather.

BULBS Plant summer flowering tigridias, galtonias, acidantheras, outdoor freesias, *Crocosmia masonorum* and nerines. Set the bulbs and corms to a depth of three times their maximum width.

Leave faded and shrivelling leaves of spring flowering bulbs to die back completely before removing them from the plant. If this job is done too early, while the leaves are green or even yellow, much of the food within the leaf will not have passed down into the bulb to strengthen it for flowering well the following year.

TOPICAL TIPS

WEED CONTROL If you possess borders in which just shrubs and roses grow, clear weeds from the soil and water on a dilution of simazine which will keep the area free of weeds for almost 12 months. The soil should not be disturbed after application. The same treatment (but a stronger dilution) can also be given to paths and drives.

SHARPEN TOOLS Shears, secateurs, knives and hoe blades should all be sharpened now before the season gets underway.

SLUG CONTROL Trap these pests in bottles (containing a little beer) which have been sunk to their necks in the ground, or by laying poisoned baits under a tile out of the reach of children and animals.

VEGETABLES

SOWING AND PLANTING GUIDE

Vegetable	Sowing/ Planting depth	Planting/ Transplanting period	Spacing between plants	Spacing between rows	Recommended varieties
Beans, Runner	In pots or boxes in greenhouse	May	15cm (6in)	30cm (12in)	Achievement, Enorma
Beetroot	2.5cm (1in)	—	10cm (4in)	30cm (12in)	Boltardy, Detroit-Little Ball
Calabrese	2cm (¾in)	May	15cm (6in)	60cm (24in)	Green Duke, Express Corona
Cabbage	2cm (¾in)	May	45cm (18in)	45cm (18in)	As March, or Greyhound, Winningstadt
Cabbage, Savoy	2cm (¾in)	July	60cm (24in)	60cm (24in)	Ormskirk, Rearguard
Cauliflower	2cm (¾in)	June	45cm (18in)	60cm (24in)	Brisbane, Barrier Reef
Lettuce	2cm (¾in)	—	30cm (12in)	30cm (12in)	As March, or Tom Thumb, Unrivalled
Onion, Salad	2cm (¾in)	—	2.5cm (1in)	30cm (12in)	White Lisbon
Parsley	2cm (¾in)	—	10cm (4in)	30cm (12in)	Moss Curled, Consort
Parsnip	2.5cm (1in)	—	10-15cm (4-6in)	30cm (12in)	As March, or Improved Hollow Crown
Spinach	2cm (¾in)	—	23cm (9in)	30cm (12in)	Sigaleaf, Perpetual (Leaf Beet)
Turnip	2cm (¾in)	—	15-23cm (6-9in)	30cm (12in)	Snowball, Golden Ball

A colourful collection of spring bulbs

May

WEATHER AND THE GARDENER

Once spring has really arrived to stay and summer is not far away, the essential ingredients for good growth are energy from the sun, plant food from soil nutrients and, most of all, soil moisture available to the roots, without which the rest are useless. Although rainfall in Britain is usually well distributed throughout the year, there often are dry spells, especially during the summer half-year, when evaporation from the soil and transpiration from the trees and plants exceed the rainfall replacement so that the soil moisture reserves decrease. To make good this deficit, gardens need watering or irrigation.

If we could only see the water used by gardens, it would be easier to realise how much soil moisture is lost to the atmosphere. At this time of year a garden will use 2.5cm (1in) of water — 24 litres per sq metre (4½ gallons per sq yard) - every 10 days on average.

For maximum growth this loss should be replaced by rainfall plus watering, to maintain soil moisture at the optimum level. It is the vegetable garden which profits most from skilful maintenance of soil moisture regimes; heavy crops cannot be grown on a dry soil.

TREES AND SHRUBS

COLOURFUL PLANTS THIS MONTH Those in flower this month include crataegus (hawthorn, may), laburnum (golden rain), malus (crabs), prunus (almonds, apricots, cherries, peaches etc.), pyrus (ornamental pear), sorbus (mountain ash), camellia, ceanothus, chaenomeles, *Choisya ternata*, cotoneaster, cytisus (broom), daphne, enkianthus, erica (heaths and heathers), genista (broom), helianthemum (rock rose), kerria (Jew's mallow), lonicera (honeysuckle), magnolia, paeonia (tree paeony), potentilla (cinquefoil), pyracantha (firethorn), rhododendrons (including azaleas), rosa (rose), clematis, lonicera (honeysuckle) and wisteria.

PRUNING Remove weak, straggly, diseased or old shoots from plants which have flowered in earlier months.

Cut, or pinch out with finger and thumb, dead flower heads of rhododendrons, azaleas and ericas (heaths and heathers).

Remove about two thirds of the length of the stems of recently planted evergreens such as cotoneaster.

PLANTING Shrubs that need the protection of a sheltered position to survive cold winters are planted now; these include *Cytisus scoparius* (broom), choisya, and some fuchsias, magnolias and hydrangeas. Water in thoroughly after planting.

FLOWERS

HARDY BORDER PLANTS Thin out congested new shoots of clump-forming plants such as delphiniums, Michaelmas daisies, phlox, solidago and lupins, to about 2.5cm (1in) apart, to encourage strong flowering stems.

Keep down weeds. Hoe them out with a Dutch or swan-necked draw hoe, when they are so small you can hardly see them. Leave them to dry on the soil surface. Deep rooting perennial weeds such as bindweed, nettles, docks and thistles are best forked out, to remove as much of the root as possible.

ALPINES Plant summer-flowering species such as achillea, anthemis, epilobium, erigeron, penstemon, thymus, veronica and zauschneria, in gritty soil enriched with bone meal.

Top dress every part of the rock garden with a gritty mix of equal parts loam, peat, sharp sand, adding a large handful of bone meal (sterilized) to each bucketful of the mixture. Spread this over the soil to a depth of 2.5cm (1in).

BULBS Plant acidantheras, *Anemone coronaria*, dormant begonias, gladioli, ranunculi, tigridias, and other summer flowering bulbs and corms. Set them to a depth of about three times their average diameter in well prepared soil.

Lift spring flowering bulbs such as daffodils, tulips and hyacinths, whose blooms have faded and where the ground is needed for summer bedding, and replant them in good soil in a spare part of the garden in full light. Lift and dry off the bulbs when the leaves have turned brown and withered.

TOPICAL TIPS

IRRIGATION SYSTEMS Soon you are going to need some form of irrigation system if the garden is not to suffer from drought. Equip yourself now with a good hosepipe and tap connector, and a suitable oscillating or rotating sprinkler with a spray pattern that will fit your garden.

HOEING Pushing a Dutch hoe through the top 1cm (½in) of soil in beds, borders and the vegetable garden is an excellent method of controlling weeds. Start this month and continue through the summer.

VEGETABLES

SOWING AND PLANTING GUIDE

Vegetable	Sowing/Planting depth	Planting/Transplanting period	Spacing between plants	Spacing between rows	Recommended varieties
Beans, Dwarf French	5-8cm (2-3in)	—	10cm (4in)	45cm (18in)	Masterpiece, The Prince
Beetroot	2.5 (1in)	—	10cm (4in)	30cm (12in)	As April, or Avonearly, Globe
Cabbage, Autumn	2cm (¾in)	July	30cm (12in)	45cm (18in)	Harbinger, Durham Early
Carrot	12mm (½in)	—	8cm (3in)	30cm (12in)	As March, or New Red Intermediate
Lettuce	2cm (¾in)	—	30cm (12in)	30cm (12in)	As April
Marrow	2.5cm (1in)	—	60cm (24in)	60cm (24in)	Zucchini, Green Bush Improved
Onion, Salad	2cm (¾in)	—	2.5cm (1in)	30cm (12in)	White Lisbon
Pumpkin (and squash)	2.5cm (1in)	—	60cm (24in)	60cm (24in)	Hundredweight, Hubbard Squash Golden
Radish	12mm (½in)	—	2.5cm (1in)	15-23cm (6-9in)	As March, or Scarlet Globe, Crystal Ball
Swede	2.5cm (1in)	—	10cm (4in)	40cm (16in)	Sutton's Western Perfection, Mancunian
Sweetcorn	2.5cm (1in)	—	45cm (18in)	45cm (18in)	First Of All, Kelvedon Glory
Tomato	Sow in pots under glass in March	May/June (18-24in)	45-60cm (18-24in)	45-60cm	Alicante, Moneymaker, Marmande

Rhododendron and *Clematis macropetala*

June

WEATHER AND THE GARDENER

June may have the longest days, and often brings the most sunshine, but it is rarely the warmest month of the summer. It can, however, be dry, and then the watering problems of May become even more serious.

The favourite way to reduce the evaporative loss of moisture from open soil is by mulching, but a mulch should never be applied too early in the season because it greatly increases the risk of a late frost, the temperature at night over a mulched surface being much lower than that over bare moist soil.

The best time to apply a mulch is probably in late May or early June.

Although a mulch will prevent light rainfall from entering the soil, it will facilitate the entry of heavy rains because it prevents the soil becoming capped by a rapid drying out on the surface. This maintenance of an open soil surface beneath the mulch also helps oxygen and carbon dioxide exchange and it prevents excessively high soil surface temperatures in hot weather.

An alternative to mulching is the frequent hoeing to remove all weeds, but this must be confined to a shallow soil layer. Deeper disturbances of the soil will increase the loss of water by evaporation.

TREES AND SHRUBS

COLOURFUL PLANTS THIS MONTH In June there is a wealth of flowers, including laburnum (golden rain), magnolia, robinia, abelia, *Buddleia globsa*, cistus (rock rose), cotoneaster, cytisus (broom), deutzia, erica (heaths and heathers), escallonia, genista (broom), hebe, helianthemum (rock rose), hydrangea, kalmia, lonicera (honeysuckle), olearia (daisy bush), paeonia (tree paeony), philadelphus (mock orange), potentilla (cinquefoil), rhododendron (including azalea), rosa (rose), syringa (lilac), viburnum, clematis, jasminum (jasmine), and wisteria.

PRUNING At the end of this month, or the beginning of next, when flowering is finished cut back the flowered shoots of deutzia, philadelphus (mock orange), ribes (flowering currant), genista and cytisus (brooms). Remove dead flower heads from rhododendrons and azaleas, ericas (heaths and heathers), laburnums (which have poisonous seeds) and syringas (lilac).

NEW PLANTS FROM OLD Layer low growing shoots of clematis and *Chaenomeles japonica* (Japanese quince) by pegging them with U-Shaped

wires into peaty soil near the parent plants. Sever and replant whe
rooted.

FLOWERS

HARDY BORDER PLANTS Use a sharp knife or secateurs and cut back to
sturdy shoots lower down flowered stems of lupins, brunnera, doroni-
cum and other early spring flowerers. Then a second show of bloom may
reward you.

Gather blooms regularly which are grown for house decorations to
encourage plenty more to replace them. This applies to astrantia,
buphthalmu, campanula, *Chrysanthemum maximum* (Shasta daisy) and
many others that produce a succession of flowers.

Spray insecticide - one of the systemic brands which stay within the
plants' systems for several weeks - to combat pests such as greenfly and
whitefly that may be colonizing soft shoot tips or leaves and crippling
growth.

ALPINES Prune back the seeding cushions of flowered aubrieta, iberis
(candytuft) and alyssum, to leave a generous centre of new shoots to
flower next year.

Carry on hoeing round larger plants not surrounded by mulches of
stone chippings to remove bittercress which is an invastive annual that
can quickly swamp the rock garden.

Dab deeply entrenched perenuial weeds such as goutweed (also called
ground elder), with a selective 'stick' weedkiller based on 2,4-D. This
will kill off the entire root system without harming the rock plant with
which it is too entangled to remove by forking out.

BULBS Dig up and dry off tulips and hyacinths whose leaves are yellow
and 'spent' and store in a cool place for the summer, before replanting in
early autumn.

Start mowing grass in which naturalised narcissi are now showing
faded, brown leaves. This indicates that all nourishment from the foliage
has been channelled to the bulbs and the leaves can now be removed.

Sprinkle a balanced fertilizer at 120g per sq metre (4oz per sq yard)
among summer flowering bulbs such as gladioli, acidantheras and
galtonia, to spur the development of strong flowering stems.

VEGETABLES

JUNE SOWINGS Further successional sowings can be made outdoors of
French beans, beetroot, carrot, lettuce, marrow (and courgette),
pumpkin (and squashes), radish, swede, sweetcorn and turnip. In

addition this is the latest time to sow runner bean directly in the open ground. These are gross feeders and the site on which they are to be grown should be prepared thoroughly, digging in compost or manure to the bottom spit of soil in a strip length of the row and 60cm (24in) wide.

POTATOES The growth of early potatoes will now be well above ground, but they should be earthed-up in stages to produce a wide flat-topped ridge. This ensures that any rain that falls on the crop will penetrate down to the developing tubers.

THINNINGS Many of the crops sown earlier in the year should now be thinned for the first, if not the second time. Thinnings from some crops, like carrots, produce useful variety for summer salads.

TOPICAL TIPS

HEDGE CLIPPING By June, most hedges have put on a fair amount of growth and need their first clipping of the year. Stretch a line along the hedge to mark the required height and clip to it with a pair of sharp shears or an electric trimmer. Large-leaved hedges, like laurel, are best cut with secateurs. Clear the clippings from beds and borders as soon as the job is finished - a hessian or polythene sheet laid alongside the hedge to catch the shoots as they fall will save a lot of time.

BIRD DAMAGE To prevent birds from decimating fruit and vegetable crops, cover the appropriate areas of the garden with plastic netting as the crops reach their most susceptible stages. As soon as raspberries turn pink they are liable to be pecked from the canes, and many brassicas are in danger of being stripped by pigeons at any time of year. Properly constructed fruit cages give the most effective protection, but they are rather expensive.

Rose 'Piccadilly'

July

WEATHER AND THE GARDENER

Although good weather and skilful gardening will encourage plant growth, there are other things which prosper under favourable conditions and are less welcome in the garden, namely, pests and diseases.

The weather is the controlling factor which determines the rapid increase of a pest or disease. Warm, dry weather seems to favour the prevalence of garden pests, although it can also accelerate the multiplication of their natural predators.

Wet and humid weather is more favourable to most diseases such as potato blight, and July is the month when spraying against blight is most important, especially if outdoor tomatoes are being grown nearby, as they are also subject to this disease.

Notice should be taken of the weather forecasts when selecting the time to spray, because it is no use applying a dust or spray to plant leaves if it is going to be washed off quickly by rain. Rain, however, can help to wash in a top dressing of fertilizer or other surface treatment.

TREES AND SHRUBS

COLOURFUL PLANTS THIS MONTH Some trees, shrubs and climbers giving a good display this month include forms of catalpa (Indian bean tree), magnolia, liriodendron (tulip tree), *Buddleia davidii* (butterfly bush), calluna, daboecia and erica (heaths and heathers), cistus (rock rose), escallonia, fuchsia, hebe, hydrangea, hypericum (St John's wort), lavandula (lavender), olearia (daisy bush), philadelphus (mock orange), potentilla (cinquefoil), rhododendron, yucca, clematis, jasminum (jasmine), lonicera (honeysuckle), passiflora (passion flower) and polygonum (Russian vine).

PRUNING Continue lightly pruning those plants which flower on the current year's growth, such as jasminum (jasmine), philadelphus (mock orange), deutzia, cytisus (broom), helianthemum (rock rose) and *Choisya ternata* (Mexican orange blossom).

HEDGE PRUNING Trim to shape any hedges that require attention, either using shears for formal hedges or secateurs for informal ones. Hedging plants usually requiring treatment now include berberis (barberry),

cotoneaster, pyracantha (firethorn), rosmarinus (rosemary), hebe, ̄
(beech), ilex (holly), *Carpinus betulus* (hornbeam), taxus (yew), ligustr
(privet), buxus (box), evergreen ceanothus, deutzia, laurus (laure
Crataegus monogyna (quickthorn), *Chaenomeles japonica* (Japanes
quince) and *Osmanthus delevayi*. Burn all prunings.

FLOWERS

HARDY BORDER PLANTS Divide overgrown and weakly clumps of
bearded irises, *Iris germanica*, and replant in well-dug soil enriched with
130g per sq metre (4oz per sq yard) of balanced fertilizer

Watch out for twisted, curled and needle-like leaves on phlox which
indicate an attack by eelworm, a pest which is microscopic and which
lives only in the stems, never invading the roots. Wait until autumn, then
dig up and burn infested plants and perpetuate your stock from root
cuttings.

Scatter a high-potash fertilizer over the root areas of plants such as
salvias and solidago which are beginning to bloom. This will accentuate
the flower colour and increase the plants' resistance to pests and diseases.

Disbud early chrysanthemums, removing all but the terminal bud on
each stem if you want large, show-quality blooms this autumn. Go over
the plants several times each season.

Save seed pods for earlier flowered aquilegias. lupins, oriental poppies
and some other plants that set viable seeds freely which can be gathered
now and sown immediately to raise new plants. Germinate them in
shallow drills 15cm (6in) apart in a humus-rich patch of ground in full
sun.

ALPINES Take cuttings of dianthus: pull out growing tips (called pipings)
and insert in pots or trays of sandy compost in a cold frame shaded from
bright sunlight. Water with a rosed can to keep the soil just moist but not
soggy.

Keep up a war on weeds, pricking over the soil with a long-handled
'hand fork'. This is a most useful tool, enabling you to probe far back
into the rock garden without treading on and damaging plants.

BULBS Plant *Amaryllis belladonna*, that spectacular late summer/autumn
flowering trumpet 'lily'. Set the bulbs with their bases 15-20cm (6-8in)
deep and resting on a 2.5cm (1in) layer of sharp sand if the soil is heavy
and inclined to lie wet after heavy rain. Groups of six or eight bulbs will
provide a breathtaking spectacle when few other bulbs are in flower.
Cyclamen coum, *C. europaeum* and *C. neopolitanum* may also be planted:
set corms about 5cm (2in) deep in peat-enriched soil. Plant in groups of
seven or nine for good effect.

VEGETABLES

JULY SOWINGS A further sowing of lettuce will provide heads in to the autumn, and turnips sown early this month will give storeable roots in the autumn given good growing conditions. Carrot and beetroot can be sown up until about the middle of the month in the south to mature before the winter, usually on land cleared of earlier crops. Make a further sowing of parsley for use in the spring.

In northern gardens, seeds of spring cabbage should be sown at the end of July for transplanting in September. If, for any reason, the garden looks as if it is going to be short of brassicas in the winter, sow spring cabbage in situ in the second half of this month.

PLANTING BRASSICAS Plant out, from seed beds, brassicas required for winter cropping - winter-hardy cauliflower, winter-hardy cabbage, kale, sprouting broccoli and savoy. This is often a difficult time to get plants established because temperatures are high and it is dry. Transplant in the evening rather than the morning, plant firmly, having scraped aside dry surface soil to expose the moist soil 5-8cm (2-3in) down. Water in plants thoroughly.

RUNNER BEANS These should be growing towards the tops of their supports and when they have reached them, the growing points should be pinched out. There is no point in leaving them to grow on as a means of producing a late crop. Plants stop cropping because beans are left to mature instead of being picked regularly.

TOPICAL TIPS

NEW PLANTS Keep an eye on newly planted trees, shrubs and other garden plants and give them a good soak when the soil starts to dry out. All plants need adequate supplies of moisture, particularly in the first year when their root system is becoming established. Pots, hanging baskets and windowboxes should be checked for water daily and soaked when necessary.

CHECK TIES As ornamental and fruit trees grow, so their trunks expand. Check that the ties that bind them to their stakes are not constricting their growth, and slacken any that look too tight.

Summer border

August

WEATHER AND THE GARDENER

August is the last month of the English summer, and indeed in Scotland it may be regarded as the first month of autumn. Its weather pattern often copies that set by July, which perhaps explains the legend of St Swithin.

If the summer has been dry, however, August is the time of great soil moisture deficits, accompanied inevitably by bans on the use of hosepipes and similar restrictions which beset a gardener as the authorities try to eke out their inadequate water supplies. Under such circumstances water has to be used with care in a garden. Certain plants or crops have to be given priority, so it is wise to find out the critical stages in their growth when plentiful soil moisture is important. Limited water supplies should not be rationed to all plants, but given to those which will benefit most.

TREES AND SHRUBS

COLOURFUL PLANTS THIS MONTH Those in flower now include forms of catalpa (Indian bean tree), eucryphia, magnolia, buddleia (butterfly bush), calluna, erica and daboecia (heaths and heathers), caryopteris, ceanothus, clerodendrum, deutzia, fuchsia, genista (broom), hibiscus (tree hollyhock), hydrangea, hypericum (St John's wort), lavandula (lavender), *Leycesteria formosa*, myrtus (myrtle), olearia (daisy bush), potentilla (cinquefoil), rosa (rose), yucca, clematis, jasminum (jasmine), lonicera (honeysuckle), passiflora (passion flower) and polygonum (Russian vine).

PRUNING Lightly clip lavandula (lavender) to remove dead flower heads. Also trim cytisus (broom) and helianthemum (rock rose).

ROSE CARE Remove flowers as they fade. Cease general rose feeding at the end of the month and apply potash at 60g per sq metre (2oz per sq yard) to help ripen the shoots for winter.

NEW PLANTS FROM OLD Use trimmed unflowered lavender shoots as cuttings, removing the lower leaves and inserting in sandy soil in a sheltered position. Take cuttings of new side shoots of heathers if required. All should be ready for final planting in 12 – 15 months time.

Layer low growing shoots of jasmine, rhododendron, viburnum and cotinus (smoke tree) by nicking underneath the stem with a knife and pegging down with a U-shaped wire into peaty soil near the parent plants. Sever the plant when rooted.

FLOWERS

HARDY BORDER PLANTS Gather statuesque stems and flower heads of blue eryngium (sea holly) and just opening blooms of catananche (cupid's dart) for drying and creating winter flower arrangements; do the same with *Physalis franchetii* (Chinese lantern).

Divide mat-forming, small leaved plants that flowered earlier, such as waldsteinia and armeria. Larger leaved plants must be left until next month. Water in thoroughly and spread moist peat among their crowns to reduce moisture loss from the root area.

Remove spent flowers from seedling perennials flowering precociously, to direct energy to strong vegetative growth and better flowers the following year.

ALPINES Take a look round your local garden centre or pay a visit to a rock garden specialist to select plants for flowering in late summer and autumn when there is little colour about. Kinds to choose include scarlet, fuchsia-flowered *Zauschneria californica,* August, September; *Solidago* 'Tom Thumb', golden yellow, September, October, and pinkish red spiked *Polygonum affine* 'Darjeeling Red', September, October.

Take heeled cuttings of *Genista lydia, G. kewensis, Thymus nitidus* and other shrubby plants: make them about 5cm (2in) long, remove the lower leaves, dip in hormone rooting compound, then insert to half their length in a rooting medium of equal parts sharp sand and peat

Container-grown conifers are not difficult to establish and there are many handsome forms to give your rock garden charm too. Some of the most interesting and shapely are golden *Thuya orientalis aurea nana,* yellow thread-leaved *Chamaecyparis pilifera aurea nana,* and the blue-green carpeting *Juniperus sabina* 'Tamariscifolia'.

BULBS Plant in groups of seven or nine, bulbs of the October flowering *Sternbergia lutea,* a beautiful giant golden crocus-like plant for a sheltered position in light shade. Set the following bulbs 5cm (2in) deep: autumn flowering crocuses such as the violet blue *C. Cancellatus cilicius,* lilac *C. goulimyi,* rosy lilac *C. sativus cashmerianus,* rich violet *C. speciosus;* daffodils for forcing into early flower for Christmas, such as variety 'Paper White'; and *Colchicum autumnale* (naked ladies) which produces its large crocus-like heads in October, but without foliage.

VEGETABLES

AUGUST SOWINGS In favoured situations make a last sowing of lettuce, specially a mildew-resistant variety, such as Avondefiance. Make a second sowing of spring cabbage in the first week of the month. Finally, make a further sowing of salad onions for use over winter and in spring.

Now is a good time to sow large onions for overwintering. These are a relatively new crop, with varieties mainly of Japanese origin. Sow on a piece of well-drained soil which has been cleared of a crop for several weeks and prepared so that moisture has come back near to the soil surface. Germination is required to start quickly after seed sowing, and for this good moisture is essential. The emergence of onions is much more rapid than in the cold conditions of spring, now taking perhaps as little as eight days.

CELERY CARE Now is the time to earth-up maincrop celery, but keep soil out of the centres of plants. Make sure that stems on outside rows of self-blanching celery beds are covered. Individual plants within the bed blanch each other by excluding light. Unless either a sheet of black polythene or wooden planks are put close up to the plants round the outside of the bed, the sticks will remain green in the light and be less attractive. Applications of nitrogen to self-blanching celery are important.

TOPICAL TIPS

HOLIDAYS If you are to go away on holiday, try to enlist the help of a neighbour to water plants in your house, greenhouse and garden, and to pick fruit and vegetable crops as they reach maturity. If no volunteer is available, take the precaution of plunging your house plants in trays of moist peat and leaving them in a shady room. The garden will have to take care of itself (mulching can help to retain moisture here) and the greenhouse can be fitted with an automatic ventilating arm and capillary benches. Leave shading on the south side of the house for the duration of your holiday.

HOEING Continue to hoe regularly in the vegetable plot and in borders which have not been mulched.

Cultivating the vegetable garden

September

WEATHER AND THE GARDENER

Although inland gales are unlikely to occur until later in the year, winds in September are generally stronger than those prevailing in the summer.

Good, carefully planned shelter from the wind is essential for successful gardening, especially in sites near the coast, on hills, or in extensive flat areas where there is little natural obstruction to the flow of wind. A hedge provides better shelter than a solid fence or wall, because it filters the wind without causing damaging down-draughts on the leeside.

TREES AND SHRUBS

COLOURFUL PLANTS THIS MONTH Those in bloom this month include *Magnolia grandiflora* and its varieties, *Aralia elata*, some buddleias, varieties of *Calluna vulgaris, Daboecia cantabrica* and ericas (heaths and heathers), various forms of hardy fuchsia, some hebes, hibiscus (tree hollyhock), hydrangeas, hypericums (St John's wort), potentillas (cinquefoil), *Genista tinctoria* (brooms) and its varieties, and certain varieties of clematis, jasminums, hardy passifloras (passion flowers) and polygonums (Russian vine).

PREPARE FOR PLANTING If a new shrub border is to be created, or individual specimen plants set out during the winter months, start preparing the sites now. Most trees and shrubs are relatively deep rooted and long lived, and to give them the soil conditions they require it is advisable to 'double dig' the planting area. Do this by removing the top soil, then fork into the subsoil well rotted manure, compost, or peat (especially on chalky soils), and apply bone meal at the rate of about 60g per sq metre (2.1oz per sq yard). Replace the top soil. Do not use fresh manure or quick acting fertilizers, which could cause root damage.

This is a good month to transplant any trees or shrubs that require moving. Choose a warm, rather wet day if possible and retain as much soil around the roots as is practical.

ROSES Prune and train ramblers and climbers, except for those which produce a second flush of flowers late in the year. With sharp secateurs, and preferably wearing gardening gloves, cut out the previous year's shoots and carefully disentangle them from this season's new growths. Cut down the old shoots to the nearest strong new growth about 45cm (18in) from the base of the plant. If there are insufficient new growths

from or near ground level, leave one or two of the old shoots but prune
back all the side growths to 8-10cm (3-4in).

Train the new stems of climbing roses, while they are still flexible, by
tying against their support with garden twine. Bending the lowest shoots
horizontally will encourage new sideshoots.

FLOWERS

HARDY BORDER PLANTS Look over herbaceous borders and dead head
where necessary; remove and clean canes from flowered plants that are
dying back; continue weeding to keep ground clean and prevent weeds
seeding and carpeting the ground next year.

BULBS Fork out spent gladioli and acidantheras. Dry off the bulbs and
foliage in a frame or greenhouse then, when the leaves are brown and
shrivelled, cut off the stems an inch or so from the top of the bulb. Set
the bulbs almost touching, in seed trays, and overwinter them in a
frost-free shed or garage.

VEGETABLES

SEPTEMBER SOWINGS Make a sowing of lettuce outdoors to overwinter
there, leaving the crop unthinned until the spring to offset the possible
effect of the winter on them. September is also the last opportunity to
sow turnips, onions and varieties of broad-leaved and curly-leaved
endive.

POTATO BLIGHT Remove the tops of main-crop potatoes if they are
affected by blight, otherwise spores will reach the tubers by washing
through the soil and they will then be damaged. Where slugs are known
to be a problem early lifting of main-crop potatoes is advisable. Outdoor
tomatoes can also be affected by potato blight, particularly the fruit.
Application of fungicides is necessary for control.

TOPICAL TIPS

TIDYING UP Beds and borders in the garden often look bedraggled and
untidy at this time of year. Clean them up by clipping away dead stems
and flowerheads, and by hoeing through the soil. Where the ground has
been mulched through the summer, the organic layer may be lightly
forked in now to enrich the soil; weed growth will be slower, rain more
abundant, and the soil will be able to give off heat more at night, so
affording the plants protection from frost.

Dahlia border and *(foreground) Fuchsia thalia*

Autumn colour at the lake, Wisley

October

WEATHER AND THE GARDENER

In autumn, not only are the days closing in, but the conditions suitable for outdoor work are getting less frequent. This means that the first favourable opportunities must be taken.

Autumn digging is important, not only because it cleans the ground of annual weeds and buries crop residues, but also because it enables the winter frosts to penetrate the rough soil surface and so break up the larger clods of earth in a very efficient manner to provide a workable tilth.

TREES AND SHRUBS

COLOURFUL PLANTS THIS MONTH Most of last month's flowers may still be providing some colour, but in addition there are a number of *Erica carnea* and *E. vagans* varieties (heaths and heathers), *Fatsia japonica* (castor oil plant), clematis, and some hardy hibiscus. Then there are the many plants which now provide us with autumn leaf colours and decorative fruits, such as some acers (maples), berberis (barberry), cotoneaster, prunus (Japanese cherries), deciduous azaleas, mahonia, viburnum and vitis (vines).

PLANTING Hardy deciduous trees, shrubs and climbers which are not container grown can be planted any time between October and March, and evergreens from October to April, provided the latter have been regularly transplanted in the nursery and are dormant when received. If there is any doubt about the state of growth or quality of evergreens, it is best to plant them this month or next, or in March and April.

Plants delivered from a nursery will either by bare rooted (no soil) or ball rooted (with soil held around the roots by sacking). Occasionally they be in pots.

When setting out a large number of plants, in a new shrub border for example, place each one at the situation it is to be planted. Work from the back, or centre, of the border or bed, outwards, so that foot marks can be removed as you plant.

SEMI-RIPE CUTTINGS Many shrubs, including *Aucuba japonica* (spotted laurel), buxus (box), deutzia, lonicera (honeysuckle) and ribes (flowering currant), can be raised now from semi-ripe cuttings. Take 30cm (12in) sturdy side shoots, trim the bases with a sharp knife below a leaf joint (or cut from the parent plant with a 'heel' - piece of bark), remove leaves from the lower half, and set 15cm (6in) deep and apart in V-shaped trenches in sandy soil in a sheltered corner of the garden.

FLOWERS

HARDY BORDER PLANTS Divide into well-rooted portions congested clumps of achillea, aconitum, alchemilla (lady's mantle), anthemis, macleaya, monarda, oenothera (evening primrose), and other vigorous herbaceous plants. Replant immediately in peat-enriched soil to spur rapid re-establishment.

Continue pruning to ground level earlier flowered plants whose seed pods are insufficiently decorative to cut and dry and use for winter flower arrangements.

ALPINES Protect woolly-leaved androsace, artemisia and other plants where autumn and winter wet can rot the foliage, by suspending a sheet of glass held up with stout wire rods, above them.

Trim back spreading plants that are swamping less vigorous kinds.

Brush fallen leaves from drabas, saxifrages, geraniums and other tiny plants in danger of being choked from them.

BULBS *Plant* muscari (grape hyacinth) beneath a hedge, to enjoy the rich gentian-blue flowers which contrast with the winter foliage or bare stems.

Continue planting tulips, daffodils and hyacinths in generous groups in the open garden, in well prepared soil, deeply dug and enriched with general fertilizer. Also, plant up outdoor containers, such as urns, vases and windowboxes.

VEGETABLES

OCTOBER SOWINGS Sow lettuce under protection to produce plants for transplanting in late November under glass to mature in the spring. Also, sow early summer cauliflower for planting out in containers and overwintering under unheated glass.

STORING ROOTS Potatoes should be lifted and left on the soil surface for a short while in drying conditions to dry them off before storing in hessian bags in a frost-free shed. Carrots, beetroot and parsnips can be stored in moist, fine soil or sand in a box kept in a shed, after their tops have been screwed off!

Parsnips can be left in the ground over winter, especially if soil is heaped over the crowns to protect them against hard frost. After March, however, they will quickly become woody and unusable.

November

WEATHER AND THE GARDENER

There is never much time available for outside garden work in November, so it is a good time to sit back, take stock, and plan ahead. For example, any garden where the average annual rainfall is 75cm (30in) or less will need serious thought concerning the maintenance of adequate soil moisture, for it is bound to suffer from checks to growth due to dry spells.

Is the garden too open to all the winds that blow, and can this be improved by the use of windbreaks? On the other hand, is it too sheltered and lacks sunshine, in which case some cutting down or even removal of the causes of shade are necessary?

TREES AND SHRUBS

COLOURFUL PLANTS THIS MONTH Although there are fewer flowering trees, shrubs and climbers at this time of year, *Prunus subhirtella* 'Autumnalis' (autumn cherry) will start blooming, also some calluna and *Erica carnea* varieties (heaths and heathers), *Jasminum nudiflorum*, (winter jasmine) some mahonias, and varieties of *Viburnum* × *bodnantense*. There will also, in a good year, still be a colourful display of autumn leaf tints and fruits from plants mentioned in October.

PROTECTING TENDER PLANTS Protect young trees, shrubs and climbers, such as some varieties of campsis (trumpet vine), cistus (rock rose), fuchsia, garrya (silk tassel bush), hebe, hydrangea and rhododendron (including azalea) which are not fully hardy until established. Use bracken or straw held in position with wire netting, twigs or pea-sticks, or by covering with polythene sheeting. Do this at the end of the month.

FLOWERS

HARDY BORDER PLANTS Fork over the soil with a border fork whose tines are smaller than a digging fork's and enable you to get in close to plants without damaging them. Take care to avoid pockets of bulbs which may have been planted.

Remove weeds while digging. Try to extricate whole lengths of tap rooted dandelions, sow thistles, docks and other deep rooters which continue to grow.

Crab apple : *Malus* 'Golden Hornet'

NOVEMBER

ALPINES Rake up carefully all rotting leaves and dying stems which can harbour slugs and snails, then scatter bait to keep these creatures from destroying the fleshy crowns of gentians and other succulent plants.

A good time to top dress with gritty compost or limestone chippings to keep the crowns of saxifrages, drabas and sedums cool and moist but not waterlogged.

BULBS Finish planting tulips. Spectacular are the lily-flowered kind in many colours. Their flared petals are magnificent and blooms are borne on strong stems to 60cm (2ft) high.

Naturalize daffodils in grass where there is less need to keep it short. Achieve a 'naturally' planted look by scattering handfuls of bulbs and planting them where they come to rest. Use a trowel or bulb planter, ideally working a litle bone meal into the hole before planting. Do the same with galanthus (snowdrops), eranthis (winter aconites) and crocuses.

VEGETABLES

NOVEMBER SOWINGS Very little to be done with vegetables now, but peas and broad beans can be sown for a May/June harvest. Choose a sheltered site - expect a few losses if the plot is cold and exposed. Grow a round-seeded pea (such as Feltham First), and go for broad beans Aquadulce or The Sutton. Cover the seedlings, and plants, with cloches.

BRUSSELS SPROUTS Take the lower leaves off sprouts and compost them. If harsh weather threatens, individual plants can be harvested complete. Remove the leaves and store the stems in a cool, dry place. The sprouts may be removed as needed for up to a week.

TOPICAL TIPS

TREE SUPPORTS Before the start of real winter winds, check that the stakes of trees are in good condition and that the ties are strong and give good support.

WATER SYSTEMS Water pipes that run through the garden above ground level should either be drained of water and the stop-cock closed, or else thoroughly lagged to prevent freezing and subsequent bursts. Draining is the safest of the two methods.

LEAVES Remove fallen leaves from all parts of the garden and place them in a wire netting pen where they can decompose. In a year or so they will have made good leafmould and can be used as a mulch or a soil conditioner.